First published 1999
by Working With Men
320 Commercial Way, London SE15 1QN

© 1999 Working With Men

Layout, Design and Printing by
RAP, 201 Spotland Road, Rochdale OL12 7AF

ISBN: 1 900468 04 2

Young, Unemployed, Unmarried...
Fathers Talking

Justin Rolph
A Working With Men Publication

1900468042.

About The Author

Justin Rolph has worked as a youth and community worker for over ten years. The last eight has been as director of the Mancroft Advice Project (M.A.P.), an information, advice and counselling centres for young people aged 11 to 25 in Norwich. The project is one of the largest voluntary sector youth information, advice and counselling centres in the country, employing 14 staff and working with over 7000 enquiries a year.

Justin has had a number of articles on different aspects of youth work published and has sat on the Youth Access National Executive since 1996.

In 1999 Justin finished an M.Ed. at the Centre for Applied Research in Education, University of East of Anglia. The M.Ed. was entitled 'Young Unemployed Unmarried Fatherhood: A Case Study' and it is the findings from this research that form the backbone of this book.

Contents

Acknowledgements

There are many people I would like to publicly thank for making this publication possible. Firstly, and most importantly, I would like to thank the young people themselves who agreed to being interviewed on tape. Their openness, honesty and humour made the research process a highly enjoyable and illuminating one for me. For this I am greatly in debt.

I would like to thank the Mancroft Advice Project for giving me the opportunity to carry out the research and in particular the Young Fathers Group, facilitated by Peter Bainbridge and Mark Osborne. This remarkable group have met weekly at M.A.P. for over five years on an almost non-existent budget. The group has struggled with getting the needs of young fathers taken seriously and I hope this book can in some small way contribute to this need.

I would also like to thank my M.Ed. Tutor, Dr. Terry Phillips, for his unstinting encouragement and advice. His interest and genuine empathy for the subject matter was central to my making the time to write.

I must thank Trefor Lloyd (Working with Men) for his assistance and for being, quite simply, one of the best trainers I have had the privilege to work with.

Finally, the start of the research coincided with my becoming a father, albeit an oldish, employed married one, for the first time myself. This personal journey heightened my interest in studying fatherhood. I must, therefore, thank my wife, Susannah, and two boys, Isaac and Jake for the shear love and joy they have brought to an otherwise cynical jaded thirty-something.

Justin Rolph

Preface

This collection of interviews explodes our stereo-typed assumptions about the men who father the babies of those teenage mothers the government is so anxious to discourage. there is nothing uncaring about the fathers interviewed here, all of them young, unmarried and usually unemployed. What we here is a mis-match of hopes, dreams and realities and quite tragic series of missed opportunities.

Andy, for example, talks with touching pride about his impending fatherhood; "Extremely chuffed about it, proof I've done something right...that I have actually got something that is going to be perfect. That's the one thing that is going to be perfect that has happened in my life."

How sad then to read later that: "He don't know me, he's five months old and he don't know who I am, they totally put me to one side. I have to see him round at her Mums because she has now got a flat and I don't know where the flat is, she won't let me know, I'm not allowed to know anything about the flat."

We don't know why the mother has chosen to cut her baby's father out of her life. What we do know is that this young man feels bewildered and hurt and that he knows, through his own experiences as a child, that is important to have two parents who will love you and stand by you.

Listening to these young men talk about their own fathers, and their feelings of loss for relationships turned sour, and fathers who were not available, it is clear that they know already, in their hearts, the importance of fathering. It would be helpful, for those in a position to make policy, to listen too, and to recognise that stereotypical assumptions about the feelings and behaviour of young men have no place in policy making.

For these young men, as much as their female counterparts, babies are not bargaining chips to be traded for state support. They are seen, above all, as a source of hope in a world with little else to offer. While it is undoubtedly true that the responsibilities of parenthood are rarely fully appreciated in advance (by mothers or fathers) these men are telling us clearly that they need no lessons in how to love their children, those working with young men need only to fan the flames that are already there. Providing support and parenthood education to young men, as well as young women, is a far more logical way to secure the future of the next generation than any campaign to stamp out teenage mothers or penalise 'feckless fathers'

Angela Phillips
author of *The Trouble with Boys*

1. Introduction

Since the late 1980s, there has been growing rhetoric about the changing state and role of the 'family'. *The Daily Mail*, in an article on one-parent families said:

'We must face the truth about these tragic children. One-parent families bring misery for parents, young people... and society.'

The Daily Mail (2/8/91)

In 1993 the then Welsh Secretary, John Redwood, and the Social Security Minister, Peter Lilley, both gave speeches deploring the increases in the numbers of teenage single mothers and of families without fathers. Back in 1971, the proportion of divorced and separated lone mothers in Britain was 4%: by 1993, this had risen sharply to 10.6% (General Household Survey, 1993), with one in five of all children in Britain living in families headed by a lone parent. Within this group, an estimated 490,000 were single lone mothers, that is women who had children without ever being married to the fathers. Teenage single mothers, the most 'controversial' group, represented about 10 per cent of this figure. These single teenage mothers, and the fathers of their children, are perhaps the people most closely associated with the current debate about the emergence of a new British underclass (e.g. Murray 1990).

Although young, unmarried mothers have been the subject of a considerable amount of research, far less has been carried out with young, unmarried fathers. This ignoring of the young, unmarried father is not new, as Bowlby, one of the most influential 20th century writers on parenting, wrote:

'The character of the unmarried father is rarely studied and not much is known of him.'

(Bowlby 1953)

Bowlby believed the opinion of experienced social workers at the time that many unmarried fathers were 'unstable' and often 'promise marriage irresponsibly'.

Throughout the 1960s and 1970s, research on young unmarried parents largely ignored fathers. Almost 40 years ago, Vincent (1960) cited the ratio of studies of unmarried fathers to studies of unwed mothers as one to twenty-five. Rhoden & Robinson (in Hawkins & Dollahite 1997) point out that it is only very recently that real progress has been made towards a fuller understanding of fathering. In particular, they argue that, until the 1980s, teenage fathers were excluded from studies on adolescent parenting and that this reflects the overall neglect of fathers in family or parenting literature. However, they go on to claim that societal stereotypes continue to depict young fathers as demonstrating their psychological maladjustment through the sexual exploitation of their girlfriends and the abandonment of both them and their children. Robinson (1988) further claims that, in the absence of information on young fathers, society has relied on the following five myths:

- **'Super stud' myth:** He is worldly wise and knows more about sex and sexuality than most teenage boys

- **'Don Juan' myth:** He sexually exploits unsuspecting and helpless adolescent females by taking advantage of them

12

- **'Macho' myth:** He feels psychologically inadequate, has no inner control and, unlike other adolescent boys his age, has a psychological need to prove his masculinity.

- **'Mr. Cool' myth:** He usually has a fleeting, casual relationship with the young mother and has few emotional feelings about the pregnancy.

- **'Phantom Father' myth:** Absent and rarely involved in the support and rearing of his children, he leaves his partner and offspring to fend for themselves.

Writing in this decade, Hudson and Ineichen (1991) continue to feed this negative picture, by stating that it is difficult to carry out qualitative research with the fathers,

'as the later stages of teenage pregnancies echo to the sound of slamming doors as the fathers make their dash for anonymity and freedom.'

(Hudson and Ineichen 1991)

In 1994, a researcher for a television documentary programme on young fatherhood rang to see if I knew any young fathers able to talk about their experiences. I found two young fathers willing to speak and the researcher interviewed them over the telephone to ascertain their suitability for the programme. Both, however, were rejected as they were considered "too supportive". When the programme was broadcast, the impression given was that the itinerant fathers who appeared were representative of all young fathers, when it was clear to me that they had been carefully hand-picked to fit this 'slamming door' stereotype.

Today in the 1990s, the issue of parenthood is extremely high on the political and social agenda, and many are calling for fresh insight. However, fathering is still under-researched according to Phares (1996). She claims that, in both published research and in unpublished doctoral dissertation research, there is an under-representation of fathers. By not including fathers in the research process, Phares believes researchers are communicating implicit messages about which parent is most integral to a child's effective functioning. She sees an urgent need for researchers and therapists to include fathers in their research and therapy. This argument had been supported earlier by Biller and Solomon (1986) in their call for a 'manifesto for research' to investigate fathers and by Robinson's (1988) demand for an increase in the quantity of studies on adolescent pregnancy that either include young fathers or focus on them exclusively. He also calls for young fathers to be researched directly, rather than using young mothers to speak for them. This book aims to provide an opportunity to hear the voices of young, unemployed, unmarried fathers and listen as they talk about their feelings, their fears and their future.

2. Interviewee Profiles

What follows is a brief description of each of the interviewees (seven young men, three young women and the five young men in the group interview) who took part in the interviews focusing on fatherhood. As well as some factual information, I have included some personal observations where I felt this added to a greater understanding of the wider context of the research. As agreed with the young people themselves, all names have been changed. Factors that might lead to them being identified have been left out or slightly altered.

Andy

His partner Claire was heavily pregnant with their first child. Knowing this, I asked Andy if I could interview him for my research project. He agreed. In an attempt to save some money for his new family, Andy had just started a summer job at a holiday camp in Great Yarmouth. This was his first paid employment for four years — he'd had a year in the army when he was 18. Andy had a 'goatee' beard, short cropped hair, wore khaki army trousers and lived in the Y.M.C.A. At the end of the interview, I asked whether I could follow up with another interview a few months after the birth to see how the reality matched up to the expectation. He agreed, but I did not see him again for many months. In January 1997, however, he came into the M.A.P. for the first time since the interview and said he was ready for the follow-up interview. This took me by surprise as I was sure he would have forgotten all about it. I fetched my tape recorder and conducted the second interview there and then, not wanting to miss the chance.

15

Dave

His partner Joanne, 16, was pregnant and expecting a baby in three weeks' time. Dave was 21, unemployed and studying G.C.S.E.s part-time at the local F.E. College. Originally from Liverpool, Dave came to Norwich for drug rehab, liked the area and decided to stay for the time being. He now lives in a council flat. He spoke with a quiet voice and has a speech impediment which meant I had to listen intently to follow what he was saying. I interviewed Dave again when he had been a father for about three months. I warmed to Dave during the interviews and enjoyed chatting to him.

Jason

Jason was 21 and had been a father for about 10 weeks. His partner, Sarah, aged 17, waited in the coffee bar with their newborn son during the interview. Jason had just started a part-time job, which, coupled with family credit, meant that they were now a little better off than they were previously on the dole. Of all the young men I interviewed, he was by far the most talkative and the most interested in reading these research project findings when finished. In December 1996, I was invited to Jason and Sarah's wedding at Norwich Registry office. I felt privileged to be there.

James

At the time of the first interview, James was 22, unemployed and living in a council flat by himself. His girlfriend Shannon lived with their daughter, Kylie aged 3 months: Shannon's mother also lived with them. James had been unemployed since leaving school at 16, apart from being on a number of training schemes: "I don't really call them proper jobs", James said. His situation during our three interviews changed rapidly and by the time of the last interview he was living in the Y.M.C.A. and had split up with Shannon.

Stephen

Stephen was 25, unemployed for the last six years and had just moved back to Norwich from Ipswich. He was living in the Y.M.C.A. Having known him for a number of years, I had seen this pattern many times before. Stephen moves on every couple of months, coming full circle back to Norwich every six months or so. On first impressions he seems like a stereotypical hippy, with his softly spoken voice, long hair and flared jeans. However, he feels himself part of no sub-culture, being very much a loner. I also interviewed his ex-girlfriend Claire (with whom he had their child, Thomas) on a separate occasion.

Peter

Peter was 24 and living with his partner, Sarah, and their two children, Jake (2) and Ben (1), in a council house. Excluding a recent job that lasted just four days, he had been unemployed for the last five years. Over some months I interviewed Peter a number of times as he preferred to talk in short but frequent slots. We shared a liking for indie music and it was easy on occasions to stray off subject.

Mick

Mick was 25 and had had two children with different partners. Other than occasional temporary seasonal work, he had been unemployed since a youth training scheme about seven years ago. With his leather jacket, numerous tattoos and his love of heavy metal music he looked hard — the sort of person many cross the street to avoid. But I observed a quiet, thoughtful person with a great sense of humour and a passion for West Ham United — qualities I rather admired.

Jackie

Jackie was 20 and living by herself in a council flat with her son Carl, who was two. Since leaving school, she had been kicked out of home, been in a number of hostels and done a couple of Y.T. schemes. Carl's father moved out soon after his arrival, and, when I interviewed Jackie, she had just discovered she was pregnant again.

Sharon

Sharon was 21 and living by herself in a council flat with her son, Wayne, who was two. Wayne's father left when he was 14 months old and hadn't been seen since. He had a 'crack' addiction, stole from Sharon all the time and used her flat to deal from.

Claire

Claire was 19 and living by herself with Thomas, her two-year-old son. Thomas's father, Stephen, who I also interviewed for this research project, was currently back in Norwich, having just returned from one of his frequent travels around the country. Claire had a refreshing honesty about herself. As a project, we supported her through her struggle with Social Services over Thomas. Her open honesty and refusal or inability to say the things and jump through the hoops required of her gave a chilling demonstration of the power Social Services hold and the fear they can strike into vulnerable people's lives. Having initially gone to Social Services for support, she spent the next year trying to release herself from their control.

Group interview

Paul

Paul was 24 and in a probation hostel awaiting trial. He had been unemployed for most of his life since leaving school at 16.

Darren

Darren was 21 and living with his girlfriend in a bedsit. Darren is a bright, lively young man with a desire to eventually get a degree. During the last couple of years, he had started a number of access courses without finishing any. At the time of the interview, he was again unemployed.

Ian

Ian was 20 and, while technically unemployed, had a number of part-time cash-in-hand jobs. One of these was with the contractors who cleaned the Benefits Agency buildings.

Colin

Colin was 21 and on restricted benefit for quitting his last job with 'no good cause'. He had no permanent address and went from friend to friend sleeping on couches. He would soon leave Norwich, only to return a year or so later having travelled most of the country.

Chris

Chris was 19 and unemployed, but with a college course in Motor Mechanics to go to in the Autumn. He was looking forward to this.

3. Fatherhood — experiences and aspirations

The first theme to be considered is the experience and aspirations of fatherhood, of which six issues were identified from the interview data.

3.1. Anticipation of fatherhood

The anticipation of fatherhood before becoming fathers for the first time, led the interviewees to worry about being able to provide.

Andy: *"Er, bit worried about making sure I've got everything, but happy."*

Jason: *"A thought went through my mind, am I going to be able to do this? Am I going to be able to do that? What about money? What about a house? And then I actually cut the umbilical cord and I must have thought more thoughts then than I had during the ten hours of labour. It was really really strange."*

Dave: *"I'm looking forward to having a family and that up here. I'm a bit daunted by it all though. I'm still not sure about it all and that but most of the time I'm looking forward to it, yeah."*

What's daunting?

"Don't know how I'm going to cope in the first couple of weeks and that, how I'm going to cope in general, you know."

A number were also concerned about how their partner coped or was going to cope.

> **Andy:** *"She just wants to get it out because the baby is causing her a lot of grief at the moment, it's getting not enough room for it. She's tired all the while and she just wants it out."*

> **Jason:** *"She often says, 'You don't know what it's like'. I said, 'I can imagine', and she said, 'No, you can't imagine what it's like to have a big lump here, you can't imagine what it's like not having sleep because of your back, you can't imagine what it's like being kicked from the inside and you'll never know what it's like to go through birth.' But at the same time she said she was glad it was her because it's an experience I'll never know and she said I should be jealous of that, which I am."*

There was an awareness that parenting can be stressful for both father and mother.

> **Dave:** *"It's easy. It can get a bit stressful, though, from time to time."*

What sort of stress?

"Just lack of sleep."

> **Mick:** *"It's stressful but its also very rewarding as well."*

What do you find stressful?

(Laughs) "The tantrums, they keep asking and you keep telling them but they don't listen. I mean, all the buying the clothes is fun but it's just like waking up in the mornings and feeding the baby when it's first born. That's the most stressful part of it."

> **Claire:** *"I do get times where I think, just go away kid, I've*

had enough, I want my life: everyone gets days like that, and then he'll smile or do something and it gives you the gumption to carry on."

3.2. Fatherhood gives a sense of pride

Fatherhood, in all the cases interviewed, led to a sense of pride and increased self-esteem.

Andy: *"Extremely chuffed about it, proof I've done something right… Well chuffed, it's a right little daddy's baby, I can't wait. It's probably going to take one look at me and go 'aarrrgh ah no'. I'm well chuffed; the day it's born I'm going to be phoning everybody."*

What does fatherhood mean to you?

"That I've done something right."

In what way?

"That I've actually got something that is going to be perfect. That's the one thing that is going to be perfect that has ever happened in my life, and that's my little un. It's like, yeah, I've done it, I'm a daddy, hurrah. I am going to be able to buy loads and loads of Christmas presents for somebody who don't even know what they mean and I'm going to be going round the city with a baby going, 'Yeah, brilliant.' Just really happy, proud."

Stephen: *"Erm, I'm chuffed at being a father, I really am, I'm over the moon about it, with Thomas now, I can see him whenever I want. Unlimited access to him and going out to see him really brightens my day up. We have a laugh with each other, he will sit down and watch T.V. with me, cuddle up to me, it really is nice to go up and see him. I really am pleased to be a father and to be able to see my son."*

Jason: *"I never knew fatherhood would be like this. The fact that he's helpless, that's a bad point in one way because you are constantly doing something for him, but then you've got the other points where you look at him and he smiles, and you look at him and he lifts his head up, or he'll realise what his hand is for, and I think, all in all, the good points outweigh the bad points. They're not bad points, more like down points. Every day that goes by, he does something new and he's leaving the helplessness behind."*

For some, becoming a father was the key motivation for living.

Mick: *"Basically, my kids are the ones that have actually got me going... I mean, basically, I really want my kids to be proud of me. I mean if it wasn't for my kids, I don't know, I'd probably get in trouble again and everything else."*

Trouble with the law?

"The law because, you know, I haven't got enough money and that. But now, because I've got the kids it's made me realise there's more to life than that. I've got to try and build a future for them. A bit of saving and that."

Stephen: *"So there's not a day that goes by when I don't think of Thomas... He keeps me going. I know that he's there and he's a great kid. Really means the world to me, he does."*

3.3. Being there for your child

There was a general acceptance of the need to be supportive to the partner and to be there for the child when needed.

Andy: *"You've got to be there for your kid. It doesn't matter what the situation is with you and the missus or whatever, but you've got to be there for the kid. I don't* *want no one else bringing up my kid: maybe that's a bad attitude, but it's my attitude, no one else could bring my kid up, so I'm going to do it permanently... my sister's in an awkward situation, she got a boy and his dad just appears when he wants to see him. He never turns up on time and sometimes never turns up at all, but that's not how I'm gonna be. If you say you are gonna be there for your kid, you've got to be there. Cos you've got to look after the kid for the rest of its life and, one day the kid's gonna look after you as well if it gets to that stage. Got to be there for your kid, got to make sure your kid's well looked after, got to love 'em. No point having a kid if you don't love 'em, might as well not be there, let someone else who does love 'em in on it."*

James: *"I've known people that have had babies and they've used them like a toy, they dress them up and that, but the novelty soon wears off. But you can't put them down because they are there for life. My dad said you're there for 18 years, but you're not because you're there for a long time afterwards as well."*

Mick: *"It's (fatherhood) like a guardian angel, someone looking over and protecting what's yours and making sure it grows up properly. I suppose it's like a farmer planting his crop, he plants the seeds and basically he just watches it grow and makes sure it grows up properly so it's ready and nice to pick. So it's like you plant the seed and watch them grow up and make sure they do the best they can."*

Several mentioned the importance of being present at the birth. In one case, this was associated with an acknowledgement of responsibility for the pregnancy.

Andy: *"Chuffed as bollocks, I was running around fucking everywhere saying 'I've got a boy, I've got a boy."*

And how would you describe that feeling?

"Er, you can't, it's just one of those ones you've just got to experience, you've got to have it happen before you know. It's really amazing, pops out this little head and it's like, 'Cor, what's that?' (laughs). You've got to be there, you can't describe it, definitely one of those. It's got to be done, if you know anyone who's pregnant and their boyfriend's a bit dodgy or their husband's a bit dodgy about going, go!"

Jason: *"Very moving. I was moved to tears when they gave Sarah the epidural. She started to cry because they had to do lots of things to her back, and my eyes started watering and that was a very emotionally charged moment. I felt very guilty because I had got her pregnant and I was putting her through this and there was a lot of guilt for the fact that Sarah had to have the baby."*

3.4. Being a good and responsible father

There was a strong feeling from all of those interviewed that the quality of life for their child should be better than their own had so far been. The issue of their own childhood arose again and again. For the majority who had very negative or little or no contact with their own biological fathers, there was unanimous feeling that they didn't want history to repeat itself.

Andy: *"My mum and dad split up when I was three and my mum's gone and married two blokes since then and I want to be there all the while for my little baby. If it ever needs me I'll be there, I don't care where I am, I'll be back...he's somewhere in Scotland, my real dad, but I haven't seen him for years and years."*
"I want to give my kid everything I haven't had. Claire will be the sensible one in that department and I'll be the one that goes out and spoils it rotten. Don't really care as long as my baby gets the best."

Stephen: "*My real father and my real mother, no I don't know them. My adopted mother and father, I know them, but, as far as I'm concerned, I haven't got any parents. From the way that they did treat me, I was hit about a lot at home by my dad from the age of about five or six when my sister was born. My dad resented me for the fact that I was taking the place of his natural children, and anything in the house that was wrong, I used to get beaten for it and everything, so there has always been resentment between me and my dad. And when I was 15, I went to school one day, came back and the house was completely empty, they had just upped and left.*"

What, without letting you know?

"*Yes. I was nearly taken into care by Social Services, but I done a disappearing act.*

"*I don't want my son to go through what I've been through, never. Fair enough, I was adopted: Thomas won't be adopted, but I don't want him going through all the stuff I went through ... So I'll give him all the help I can. I do not want him at all going through what I went through... I don't want to put myself about and let him think I'm being a right arsehole to him by being too stern, but, then again, I want to be firm that he knows but without going through all the heartache that I done. I don't want him to resent me after a while the way I did with my dad. That's one thing I don't want.*"

Jason: "*I thought, 'I'm now a parent', and I always thought my parents did things wrong and Sarah's parents made a real mess of her because she has still got problems dating back... and I thought to myself, 'How would I feel if that happened to me? How would I feel if I pushed my child away?' And I made up my mind that I was going to be a good parent.*"

26

Peter: *"I was in care from the age of 10 up till 16 and then made the big mistake by going home... he (father) left when I was four and my sister was three."*

And have you seen much of him since?

"We saw him at my grandfather's funeral which was quite amusing. Have you ever seen a 50-year-old aunty pole vault over four gravestones at one time?"

So you've hardly been in contact since he left?

"Oh, apart from the day he actually drove me all the way to the city when I got kicked out and he didn't know who I was!"

You were hitch-hiking?

"I was hitch-hiking and he drove me all the way to the city and dropped me off outside St. Edmonds (hostel) and he never knew who I was."

How did it feel sitting there?

"It honestly felt hilarious. I even had my name tattooed on my arm!"

Were you talking in the car?

"No, well he did say he used to work in Hinham and stuff, but that was about it."

So you have very little feeling towards your father now?

"Sperm donors, I think they call them now. He had no real effect on the way we were brought up."

Do you have any anger towards him now?

"No, I think he's a joke actually, an irritating little person."

So, at age 10, could your mother no longer cope?

*"Well, I actually did feel sorry for her a bit because she had
a breakdown and stuff and she did have four of us. I think
the best thing she ever did was to put us into care. I think a
lot more of my foster parents, like if anything ever really
went wrong, I could just go back and see them. If I needed
a bed for the night, there would be one. It's not like it's
written down or nothing. Their grandmother was related to
my step-father in some way, and they know what my step-
father was like."*

For some young fathers, their understanding and definition of
fatherhood was clearly shaped by their own experiences.

Peter: *"Basically, looking after the family and being in
control, making sure they are brought up correctly, well to
your (pause)... you go for the standards you have been set,
and you try and aim a bit higher."*

James: *"I get on with my step-dad, and I sort of get on
with my real dad. But I was young and it all happened
when I was young. But I had to get adopted through the
court when I was about six or seven. I mean, it's not a nice
experience and that's what I don't want Kylie to go
through...*

"Some of it was happy (his own childhood), *but I can't
really remember a lot about it. What I can remember was
nasty and that. That's why I really wanted to try with my
daughter and that, cos I don't want her to have the
upbringing I had, but it just seems her mum's doing it for
her. I always said, like, if I had children and that I would
make sure they were better brought up than I was."*

**And your relationship with your own father, did you
know him at all?**

Mick: *"Yes I did, unfortunately."*

So it wasn't a good relationship then?

"No, not at all."

Do you still see him now?

"The last time I saw him I was 14, but if I saw him now I would probably punch his lights out."

Because of what he did to you when you were younger?

"Because of what he did to me and my family, yeah."

So, at 14 he left your family?

"No, he left us when I was seven and my mum remarried."

Has he had a large impact on your life?

"Yes, he's really messed me up, but since I've had my first child, then it made me realise there's more to life than being like he was, hurting people. It started to change me."

The young mothers interviewed also had negative experiences of their own fathers.

They too did not want this to be repeated with their own child.

Jackie: *'My mum left my real dad when we were young, and, like, I was pretty close to my real dad, and we left: all I knew was that we were going to go on holiday with nanny for a while, and we never went back. And I don't want that for Carl."*

So you never went back home?

"No, we never went back home, cos mum just packed our stuff up and said, 'We're going to go and stay with nanny for a while'. Because we were so young, we didn't understand what was going on. I was about three, and then

we never went back to see daddy again and I don't want that happening to Carl. Cos now Paul's around and we're not getting back together, but, if Paul gets married or has other kids and that, then Carl is still going to know that daddy loves him, that Carl is still daddy's baby. Same as if mummy gets married, then mummy and daddy aren't going to stop loving you just because we've got somebody else."

Sharon: *"I grew up with a step-dad and he used to be horrible to me and I wouldn't ever want my boy to go through that."*

Claire: *"He (father) was in the army. He drunk a lot and he hit a lot, basically for anything."*

So you never had a good relationship with your father?

"No, he'll try every now and again to get a relationship going, but we can't — it's too late. But I don't like the idea of Thomas not having a grandad, so we still try purely for Thomas's sake."

Being a father led some of those interviewed to feel more mature. They also claimed they were now more responsible as they had to ensure that the child has a reasonable start in life.

Dave: *"It just makes me feel a bit old."*

A bit old?

"Yeah."

In what way?

"Well, I'm a parent now, it just makes me feel old, you know. But I've got used to it, I'm quite a domestic sort of person, I'm good at washing and any stuff like that... It often doesn't occur to my girlfriend if we've got to get this or

get that, so I have to take control. To be honest, I'm more responsible now because I've got Matthew and that."

James: *"You know, I've had my fun sorta going out and that, and they say that babies change you and that, and they do."*

Andy: *"I've been living on my own doing what I feel like. Since the baby's due to arrive, I've grown up a helleva lot, so mostly the baby's having a decent effect on me."*

Some of those interviewed showed this feeling of responsibility in an attempt at shared parenting.

Dave: *"My girlfriend doesn't like the early morning things, so I do that... Well Joanne, she doesn't do the feeds at night, I do, but during the day we generally take it in turns. But I find I take Matthew out for walks all the time, well not all the time, but quite a bit of the time: it helps him if he's starting to get a bit grizzly, helps him settle down a bit, but I enjoy taking him out for walks. I usually go on a big mad hour-long walk to the chip shop, but the chip shop is really only about two minutes walk away! ... My girlfriend gets a bit jealous because our little 'un seems to prefer me to her. If he's grizzling, he can come up to Joanne and he stays grizzling, but with me he stops straight away. I don't know why, it's just one of those things, isn't it?"*

Why do you think it is?

"I don't know, maybe it's because I take him out for more walks and that, plus I pick him up and give him a cuddle when he's not crying, cos, like, that way the cuddles and affection are unconditional. Otherwise he would cry just to get a cuddle, and would learn that that's the only way to get attention. I'm getting a bit airy-fairy aren't I? I just think it's worth it for the smiles really."

31

Peter: *"For the first three months, I basically looked after Jake because my girlfriend was still in a daze."*

Jason: *"I have to support Sarah when she's upset. I hate it, but I can't show when I'm upset as well. But I can see that she needs someone who's strong for her, and, if I need someone that's strong for me, I can see my mother, or one of my brothers.*

"What we usually do with money is we'll have spending money left over and we'll split it between the three of us. The baby will have exactly the same as me and Sarah but, most of the time, me and Sarah end up spending about half of our money on him. That gives you a good feeling. When I buy something that I can see him wearing, it gives me a content feeling. This month, I've worked out we've got about £100 and we're going to spend about £80 on him and it doesn't bother me."

3.5. Contact with child

The importance of contact is frequently mentioned, with regret being expressed when contact is reduced or lost. Problems with contact often arise when there is conflict with the partner or partner's family.

James: *"Like my girlfriend's mum and that, she doesn't really like us now. It seems to me that she only wanted me to be there until my girlfriend had Kylie and then just pushed us away and everything… And I can't see her cos she's still living at home."*

(On his feelings about being rejected by his partner's mother):
"Pardon my French, pretty pissed off actually. I mean, it wouldn't be so bad if I was some sort of junkie or womaniser or something like that that would abuse the

situation. Some people I know, like, that have children, they don't actually want to see the children, but I do and that's sort of the bad thing about it. I mean, I'm not a bad lad or nothing, I mean I'm always sort of helping somebody and that."

...So how much contact do you get with your daughter?

"Not as much as I want, but sometimes two or three times a week if I'm lucky. But when I do get to see her, it isn't what I'd call, you know, how can I put it, at ease because there is always somebody else around. I mean, I'm sort of bonding but it's not the proper sort of bonding. And I'm always worrying what people think and whatever. I mean, some people say, 'Have you got any children?' and I say, 'Yeah, I got a daughter' and they go 'How's she doing?' and I go, 'I don't know cos I don't see her', and they go 'Why not?' and I go, 'Cos I'm not allowed to', and they jump to conclusions and that. And really it's nothing I've done. Some people might think he's just got some girl pregnant and he don't care, which is totally wrong.

"...When I see her, I don't really know what to do because I think, if I try and do too much, she is going to get attached, and, if I don't, she is going to think I don't care, so really you can't win. In a way, I've just got to let her get on with it and try and forget all about it."

Stephen (on his feelings about losing touch with his first child): "Er, very upset. I walked out on my job and everything and I just felt very disheartened. We were both looking forward to it and her parents didn't like me, and she was living with her parents and they just upped and left and she went with them.

"It can be painful (loss of contact), yes, for the fact that I've never seen her. All I know is that the radio was playing

33

when she was born and the song that was playing at the time was 'Kayleigh' by Marilion so they named her Kayleigh, which is now one of my favourite songs."

Mick: "I've got the opportunity to be a good father to my son, but my daughter I haven't seen for, like, nearly three and a half years, so …"

How does that make you feel?

"It's very upsetting because I see her in the street up the city, but every time I go near her, her mother turns round, or her Nan turns round, and gives me dirty stares, so I can't go near her."

(On why he lost contact in the first place)
"I had contact with her for the first six months, but it went downhill from there. I tried, but basically the mother (ex-partner's mother) just wanted to take over… it wasn't actually the mother, it was actually the family that was sticking their nose in and trying to run things and that. It just got too much for me in the end."

Andy: "I'm one of these people that thinks that a baby has his mother, his father. They should be together for the baby: one is as important as the other. I mean, he don't know me, he's five months old and he don't know who I am, they totally put me to one side. I have to see him round at her mum's because she's now got a flat and I don't know where the flat is, she won't let me know, I'm not allowed to know, I'm not allowed to know anything about the flat."

(On his feelings about losing regular touch with his child):
"Annoyed, cos I want to see him, like, cos I'm his dad, as much as I can. When we were together, she said 'If we ever split up, however bad it's been, you can see him as much as you like' and all sorts, and what happened to that (despairing laughter)? 'No matter how we finish, whether

34

it's bad or good, you can see him whenever you want' — it just didn't happen... She won't let me take him anywhere cos she thinks I'm going to run away with him.
I mean, I couldn't do that to her because I've seen it done to my sister, so I couldn't do that to her. It's just not on."

How would you describe how you feel at the moment?

"Well, it's not fit for publication anyway (laughs). Just really pissed about it basically, just don't like it. I should be sitting there looking after my son, taking him out. I suppose, if I could take him out for days, that would be better, I wouldn't feel as bad, but it's a no-win situation for me. She's the mother, she gets all the priority, I can't do nothing. A pity really, to say the least. One day, I'll get to see him every day and take him out and about and do things with him like a normal dad should do. Like, you get all these women and they say, 'Oh, his father didn't want to know', when it's probably more than likely that they split up on bad terms and the mother didn't want the father to know. And, like, the father did want to know, but wasn't allowed near."

It was not only the fathers who mentioned the importance of their contact with the child. All the mothers interviewed noted the emotional impact of loss of contact on their children.

Jackie (after the father of her child went into prison): *"He got bad. That was a couple of weeks ago. He wouldn't go to bed without having a photo of daddy. Mummy had to give daddy a kiss and Carl had to give daddy a kiss and say, 'See daddy soon' and then I'd say, 'Lie down and go to sleep and we'll see daddy in the morning,' and then he'd sleep. He'd also have to have a dummy as well otherwise he wouldn't sleep, for like a comfort thing. He hadn't been on a dummy since he was not even a year old, but he just went* back on it again. But I thought, 'I can't deny him the dummy because he's missing his daddy. He wants his picture of his daddy and he wants comfort'."

Sharon: "When his dad did go, I didn't think it would affect my little boy, but he stopped eating, he stopped sleeping, he was just calling 'Dada, dada, dada'. He knew something was gone, he just knew it wasn't happy."

Claire: "He screamed a lot. He cried, it didn't matter what I did, Thomas just cried his eyes out, but now I don't actually think Thomas knows that Stephen is his father. I think he mostly remembers that there was a figure there and that figure isn't there anymore. I don't know how it works, but that's how I think any way."

The mothers also indicated that they missed the support of a father in parenting their children.

Jackie: "I think that they (sons) can bond more with fathers. Like, yeah, it's o.k. with the mum, but they can't always explain to little boys what little boys do, so in a way it would be better coming from a daddy... I try really hard, but you need a break from them, you need someone else to look after them for a while and explain things to them. And then they get the male side as well as the female side. I think they grow up better like that as well."

Sharon: "I miss him, I miss not having someone about, but all the decisions I've had to make I've had to make by myself. Like, with his operations for his face, because there was a chance that he could go blind, but I had to make that choice because I thought it was for my son's sake, and I had to make it by myself and it was really hard."

Claire: "I believe that, when a kid grows up, there should be a mum and dad, always. While a lot of single mums get thingyed against, I don't know what the word is—

prejudiced?

Is that the word that means like the whites towards the blacks?"

Yes, that's right.

"A lot of single mums get that, which I don't agree with. So I think there should always be a father, because it's not fair on a kid growing up on his own, basically. Yeah, he'll always have the mum, but, with the father being there, the work of bringing the kid up will be more enjoyable. The mum would get a break, and so would the dad, and the mum and dad could support each other."

...And that's what you miss the most?

"Yeah, the support from somebody else. It's one thing your mum saying you're doing a really good job, but, when Thomas's in bed and you're sitting on the settee, you've got no one to cuddle up to, do you know what I mean, It sounds kinda soft really but sometimes, and only sometimes, I take it out on Thomas. I don't mean it, but I'm like, when I try to describe this, most people say 'You hate your son'. My sister tells me this all the time, but you don't, you're just lonely. And yeah, you can cuddle up to Thomas, but you can't have a conversation with Thomas. I think all single mums, I don't think anyone would actually say this, but all single mums need someone, a special person in their life and not just the child. Many single mothers have this macho image, 'Oh I don't need anyone' kind of thing, but I reckon, if you were to get a camera into their home or where they were staying, you would see them cuddling up to a pillow or something and watching sloppy movies, cos I do that. That's what you'll find a lot of single mothers doing — and single fathers, cos there's some of them about."

3.6. Perceptions of good parenting

Interestingly, both the mothers and fathers interviewed thought that fatherhood was important. Many of them indicated that they really wanted a more conventional family structure.

> **Jason:** "To tell the truth, when Sarah suggested having a baby, that's what I've always wanted to do. I've always wanted to settle down and have a family, and I knew I was going to settle down with Sarah because, as soon as we met, I know it sounds strange, but it was love at first sight, we just clicked. I knew for a fact that I was going to stay with her, and we started talking about babies and I thought that this is exactly what I want."

> **James:** "Well, really there ain't much chance of it but, if I come into some money, one way or another, like if I win the lottery or something but I don't do it, I just want enough. So I could have me own house, nothing big, like 3 or 4-bedroomed house, married, like, to me girlfriend and that and then everyone on speaking terms, like, happy again like it was before. And, like, Kylie, like, really looked after well and stuff, and me working or something. You know, I just want in a way 2.4 children. In a way, like, I want the family to be like one of those T.V. families, with everybody smiling and that, but that isn't the real world, is it?"

> **Jackie:** "I think they need both parents; not one parent can be a mum and a dad. The same as if the dad's got the kids, you can't be a mum as well as a dad."

> **Sharon:** "I mean, if I could have a daddy for my little boy, I'd give my left arm but I have to do both jobs… I never chose to be a single parent, I became one, do you know what I mean?"

> **Claire:** "I think there should be a father, I think there should always be a father, but it doesn't always work out that way."

However, despite saying that they felt their children would benefit from having a father in the home, each of the mothers felt they had no choice in being left by themselves.

Jackie (about the father): *"He was there for about two months but, because Carl was so little, he couldn't handle it."*

What couldn't he handle?

"I think it was more of a shock to him than anything, and I don't think he was ready to have a baby yet. I don't think he could handle it at all. So he moved out and everything got sorted out and he now has Carl three days a week, and he's happy with that and Carl's happy with that."

Sharon (about the father): *"He's (the son) now two and he left when he was only 14 months. He just disappeared out of Norwich and hasn't seen him since, so my little boy wouldn't know who he was… If his dad did come back and want to see him, I'd never stop him, but it would have to be on my terms. Cos I've brought him up and I keep picking the pieces up… The thing was, he was a smack head and he kept taking from us and he was no good for us anymore. He just let him down, so…"*

What, he stole from you?

"He stole from us all the time. He sold half the stuff in my flat and took money from me and my little boy. He was never there, you know what I mean, he just let us down so. This was the fifth time he went. He left us the first time, he came back, he went and he came back and he went and he came back, and then he just went and I haven't seen him since."

So, you let him come back five times?

"Yes, but it was for my little boy's sake. I did try really hard, but it was no good anymore. I think he realised he was no good for us anymore and that is why he went, do you know what I mean, and I just accepted it."

Claire: *"Stephen walked out when Thomas was 6 months old and I've been on my own with Thomas ever since. He shows an appearance, but he doesn't stick around for long and he's, like, short tempered"*

Although the mothers wanted a 'father' for their children, they were doubtful about their children's real fathers' abilities to play the role satisfactorily.

Claire: *"In an ideal world I'd like Thomas to have a father, but — nothing against Stephen — I wouldn't want it to be Stephen, because he hasn't got the patience, do you know what I mean?"*

During both the group and individual interviews, there was some discussion of male and female roles. For the majority of the interviewees, there was a feeling that it was no longer appropriate to draw distinctions.

Group Discussion

Chris: *"The other thing is, it's always been said that women are better parents, you know, better mothers. Basically, mothers are better than dads in the sense of looking after kids right."*

Paul: *"Yeah, but they've got the instinct built in, like."*

Chris: *"Yeah, but even then it's not always true. Blokes have got the same instinct, it's just that a lot of blokes have got too much pride to actually show it. To show that they've got the motherly side of life, which is true. Every bloke's got it."*

Darren (mockingly): *"Get in touch with your feminine side."*

(Laughter)

Chris: "I mean, my dad, he was a brilliant bloody father, he looked after me and me brother for about 7 years. Supplied the food, supplied the clothes, made everything right for us and stuff like that. He was better than half these bloody women I know that reckon they're brilliant mothers and stuff like that and yet it's always 'Women are the best mothers and men are the best workers'. And yet, they want the equal rights and they want women to be the best workers and men to be the best husbands, and yet they still slag us down and say they're better than everything."

Sharon: "I mean, most of my friends, they fell pregnant just to keep their man about and it don't work... And most of them said they were getting married to get the house sorted, but I don't want that. It's not just the man's job to do the hard work, it's a two-way thing. You both have to work at it."

Claire: "I don't believe that a mum's got one special thing she can give to a kid and the father's got another. The father can give the same things that the mother can, apart from breast feed."

Mick: "I mean basically, yeah, in the 90s, as far as I'm concerned, men and women are all the same. I mean, I can do all the housework, and that, because I've been living in my own place for so long; it's just like a routine. Get up, do the housework, go out. I'm not bothered about sexist crap anymore, it's just something that has been brought up through the years and is just unnecessary."

Andy: "Blokes get hurt just as easily as women, but no one sees that apart from other blokes, which is really annoying."

4. Being unemployed

The second theme to be considered is the impact of unemployment on young fathers, of which six issues were identified from the individual interview data.

Contrary to popular myth, most unemployed, unmarried fathers interviewed had a desire to work. Mick, reflecting the feelings of the majority, said:

> "It's personal satisfaction. Instead of signing for it, you've actually gone out there and earnt it... It is boring, sitting on your bum all day just waiting for the fortnight to come and sign your name and get your money. And it isn't really worth being branded, you know, because you're on the dole, that's it, you know... We're not all bums on the social — some of us do have direction."

4.1. Financial concerns

Not surprisingly, the financial implications of being unemployed were uppermost in many of the fathers' minds. For a number, it was deeply worrying.

> **James:** "I want to help Shannon out, but I can't cos I haven't the money to give her and that annoys me. It's really painful to try and explain how I feel, cos I'm so confused about it and everything, but, at the end of the day, I can't do nothing. I get stressed out, but I take more worry on than I should do. It's silly, but it goes on."

> **Andy:** "Not having the money, that's the main worry, not having the money to give the baby everything, but, other

than that I'm like, 'Yeah!'. That's what's worrying me, coming off this job (temporary summer post) and not being able to afford to buy the baby everything it needs or wants. I don't want to get like that, I really don't."

For others, there was the frustration of wanting to work but not being able to find work paying enough so that they could financially support their families.

Peter (talking about his main hope): *"That one day I'll actually get a decent job. One that actually pays and one that has good prospects of something decent at the end of it, basically."*

So, that search for a quality job is what keeps you going?

"Yeah, something decent for a change. Not getting paid bad money. Something like the money I used to earn when I was at work... But now it's terrible, they think they can pay you what they want, and everything's part-time now. You constantly get pushed into lower paid jobs."

How does that make you feel?

"Well, it's no good for me, cos I've got two kids. You don't want part-time jobs, you want something that is going to make you feel that you can support the kids... I recently worked for 4 days, it was £2.87 for night shift for doing 9 hours. Now, when I was 18, I was getting £250 per week for sitting in a lorry all day doing nothing. Well, I was working, but most of the time doing nothing. There's more of a market for people employing people than for people trying to find employment, while, when I was younger, it was more the other way around. Now what you need is experience, but how can you get experience if you can't get a job in the first place?... Maybe there will be a time when people are able to get jobs, but I can't see it for a long time

unless something changes. Maybe they'll do what they did during the depression, start another war. There just isn't enough work. I hope that I will eventually get a job, I can't do what I used to do because of an injury. Something decent, something worthwhile."

Mick: "I hope to get a job eventually, but it's a bit hard at the minute."

So a job is important to you?

"Yeah, it's important to me, cos I've realised that you can't support yourself and two kids on basically all the money the social give yer. So..."

How does that make you feel?

"Pissed off. I mean, I've got a job if I want it, but the wages isn't enough to, is just enough to support a single person, let alone a single person with two kids as well, so hopefully I'll go to college to get me degrees and that so that I stand a better chance of getting a job."

One young father who managed to get a part-time job found his family financially better off, but only just.

Stephen: "We get family credit. When I went to the D.H.S.S., they told me I'd get about £13, so I wasn't sure about taking the job, but, when I got the family credit, I'm actually getting £51, so it was worth taking the job. Also, I get housing benefit and council tax benefit and cheap milk, not free milk."

So you're better off than you were on income support?

"To a point — roughly between £5 and £10 per week better off."

A number of the fathers were making financial contributions through the Child Support Agency. While this meant that they were often in great financial difficulty, there was a general feeling that they should contribute something.

> **Andy:** *"I'm on suspended benefit. C.S.A. are taking £9.60 off me, which is a lot out of what I've got, but I don't care – he's my son, they can have what they want. I don't care – he's my son, I just want to see him."*

4.2. Budgeting on a very low income

Many of those interviewed had had to learn to make tough decisions to live within their limited budgets.

> **Peter:** *"My main rules are I pay the electric, I pay the rent, any other bills that have to be paid off, I get the nappies and then I get the food. And then, whatever money's left over, that's what we have to play with. We're lucky because we have a large fridge-freezer, so we can buy everything in bulk.*
>
> *"Money does get a bit tight; you get days when, just before your giro turns up, you think, 'God, I could really do with a cigarette', but you manage."*

> **So it's about staying within tight budgets?**
>
> *"Yes, if we go out it's every once in a while, or buy a bottle of wine or something and sit at home and drink it, or invite a friend round and watch a video."*

> **Andy:** *"I look at it like this, the baby's nearly here, the baby needs stuff, fine, I'll cut down on everything I normally have..."*

> **Is that a change in you?**
>
> *"Yeah, normally I'll go out and blow a giro. If I got it on a*

Saturday, by the Monday I'd have no money left and that didn't bother me, but now, 'Ahhh, the baby...'"

Living on such a small amount of money has led a number of those interviewed to either maximise their benefit income or defraud the Benefits Agency, whichever way one chooses to look at it.

Dave: *"Officially, we don't live together, but unofficially we do, for benefits and what not."*

So that you can claim from separate addresses?

"Yes, we've both got our own flats at the moment, but my girlfriend is 99% of the time round mine."

And would you want to move in?

"I'd want to, but the money wouldn't be as much as we would have on our own and then I can chuck out more stuff for the baby, make sure the baby has got everything."

So for financial reasons?

"Yeah, I'll live in my own place, probably stay round hers a fair bit. I'd want to live round there, but, what do they call it, it wouldn't be financially clever. I just want to keep the money coming in."

4.3. Not reaching others' standards

A number of young fathers felt that they had been rejected by their partner's family because of their unemployment status. They felt they were being solely judged by others on their ability to bring in a wage.

James: *"That was, like, a big disappointment, like, you know, you got a child and that, but you can't see 'em and that, your partner's mum's sort of being very funny an' that* *and not letting you see it ...the reason she sort of don't want me being about is to do with the fact that I'm not working. I don't fit her standards.*

Another father felt that he had not yet reached the standard of being a 'man'.

Mick: *"I'm not a man, I'm just a boy in a man's shell, and I'll always say that, yeah, cos what does make a man? You know what I mean."*

What do you mean by boy in a man's shell?

"I mean I haven't grown up, I haven't proven myself to be a man, you know."

And how today do you prove yourself to be a man?

"...It's to do with your parents, myself, that's what I think. Your father says you're a man if you do this, you're a man if you go out and earn a crust and bring it home."

4.4. Feeling discriminated against in the job market

For those that had experience of the job market, there was the feeling that many of the traditional 'working class' jobs had disappeared and that their skills were of little use in today's job market.

Peter: *"Most of the industries I've worked in have been battered over the last few years."*

Some felt stuck in an unemployment rut.

So how long have you been unemployed?

Mick: *"On and off, about six years now. I mean, I've had jobs, seasonal work and that, but, you know what I mean... I try to go on courses, but some of the courses*

47

*aren't up to my standards, cos half the stuff I've done
already and I want to find a course that will suit me… With
me, it's just that I've been stuck in the same kind of work.
I want to broaden my horizons and try something
different… I must admit there is enough work out there for
me, but I haven't got the qualifications to say I've done it.
You know, I think that's half my problem: I've got the
experience, I know I've done it, but I haven't got the piece
of paper to say I'm qualified for it."*

The issue of discrimination had been raised during the group
interviews.

Darren: *"I think, 'I'm not against women's lib,' but I think
this women's lib stuff has gone way over."*

Paul: *"It's gone way too far."*

Darren: *"Because if you went for a job now, yeah, and
there was a woman there and you were there, I'm not
saying in all cases, yeah, and there was a male
interviewer…"*

Paul (interrupting): *"The woman would get it."*

Darren: *"The woman would probably get it, because the
bloke interviewer would be more concerned that he would
get done because…"*

Paul (interrupting again): *"Equal rights."*

Darren: *"The equal rights, and then there's still women
complaining that they're still not getting paid jobs."*

Chris: *"Cos all the woman has got to do is go and
complain somewhere with the equal rights side of things, and
they'll go down there, cause World War Three at the place
she went for an interview, and they'll think, 'O my God we*

should have given her the job, we'll give you the job now to shut everybody up.'"

Paul: *"Yeah, us blokes don't even get a look in now do we?"*

Chris: *"So many things are being blown out of proportion now."*

4.5. Confusion over male and female roles

For some young men, there is clearly conflict and confusion between the roles they feel are appropriate for men and women and the reality of their situation. This is demonstrated in the following extract from the group interviews.

Paul: *"I've always thought that the bloke should earn the money and the woman sits there, fine she doesn't have to do the housework, but the bloke gets the money. But it ain't like that anymore: Claire's working, I'm not — we got a little un on the way, and I feel such a cunt that I'm not getting the money for the little un."*

Chris: *"Yeah, cos when you've been brought up thinking that's the old-fashioned way and stuff like that, and you're the one that's ended up at home while the woman's out working and stuff like that, it does make you feel bad, even though times are changing."*

Darren: *"There's no pride left."*

Paul: *"No. I ain't ever worried about Claire working but I want to work.*

Darren: *"It's not pride as in, 'Oh I'm a big macho imbecile that goes out and gets pissed every night and kicks somebody's head in.'"*

Paul: *"That's not what it's about though, is it?"*

Darren: *"It's not. You've always been brought up…"*

Paul: *"Where the bloke earns all the money."*

Darren: *"Yeah, where the bloke earns the money, and stuff like that. I don't mind it if the wife goes out and earns the money and that lot, it's just that it's always been that the bloke done it."*

Paul: *"I reckon that the bloke goes out and gets the money for the family. The woman goes out if she wants to go to work; she goes to work and gets the money for her."*

Darren: *"There would always be her money. Like, if I went out and earnt money now, my money would be spent on bills, stuff for the babies, food and other things, and whatever money she earned is hers. As long as there's always money there to pay bills I'm not concerned."*

So, why's there no pride now in being a man? Is it because there is no work?

Paul: *"Well, there's no work, and, if there is work, most women do get the job like Chris said."*

Chris: *"And also another problem is, the opportunity for a man to be what a man has always been classed as has been taken away from us. If we try and act like that, we get slagged down, we get nagged at and we get all these women bitching at us, and all we're trying to do is do what men have been doing for thousands of years, looking after their home, looking after the women, you know, looking after their wives, sort of thing, and looking after the kids and supplying. If the woman wants to go out and do a bit of work, fine, I've got no problems with that. But the reason we haven't got much pride left in that sense is cos it's all*

50

been taken away from us. If we try and say, you know, 'I'd like to do the work and bring in the money and all that", you know, they moan, sort of thing. But what they don't seem to understand is, it's something we've been doing for thousands of years, and we've been bloody good at it."

For others, however, the changing work climate for men and women held no such difficulties.

Mick: *"I mean basically, yeah, in the 90s, as far as I'm concerned, men and women are all the same. I mean, I can do all the housework and that because I've been living in my own place for so long, it's just like a routine. Get up do the housework, go out. I'm not bothered about sexist crap anymore, it's just something that has been brought up through the years and is just unnecessary."*

So, if you were living with your partner, you wouldn't mind who went out to work?

"No I don't care, as long as there's a meal on the table, if you know what I mean. It doesn't matter if I do it or whoever, basically, as long as the family is up and running."

4.6. Positive aspects of unemployment

Whilst, clearly, unemployment was almost entirely viewed in negative terms, one young father felt it should be compulsory for all new fathers.

Peter: *"I think everyone should be made unemployed for six months after a baby's been born."*

Why's that?

"So that then they know damn well how hard it is."

For other fathers, their unemployment meant that they could take a more active role in supporting their partner and children.

> **Mick**: *"I go to the Y.M. and use the foyer, trying to find work. But it's hard, cos I've got to look after the kids as well as Julie. I hope to get a job eventually, but it's a bit hard at the minute."*

One young father specifically took a part-time job so that he could spend more time with his son.

> **Stephen:** *"That suits us down to the ground, because I only work from 8 till 1, so most of my time is still spent with my kid."*

While another gave up a part time job to be more supportive at home

> **Dave:** *"I got a job recently and had to give it up because Joanne just couldn't cope on her own. I think she was having a nervous breakdown at the time, and so I had to come home and look after the baby and that. One time I came back and she was just sitting there looking after Matthew and trying to get out of her head. She just wanted some stress relief and that, and the baby was crying, so I had to look after him and that."*

5. Being unmarried

The third theme to be considered is the impact of being unmarried on young fathers, of which three issues were identified from the interview data.

5.1. Legal issues

An unmarried father has no automatic parental responsibility for his child. He can only acquire parental responsibility by making a formal agreement with the mother, by obtaining a court order, by becoming the child's guardian (which would only take effect on the mother's death) or by marrying the mother. He is not presumed to be the father of a child.

Some of the fathers interviewed were aware of this legal situation and knew that they had no automatic parental rights because they were unmarried.

> **Andy:** *"Officially, I've got no rights whatsoever."*

> **Dave:** *"I got very little, or no, rights over the kid unless Joanne agrees to sign."*

Group discussion

> **Darren:** *"You've got nothing unless you're married. Like there's, urm, parental responsibility and that lot."*

However, others felt that there wasn't enough information available on this issue.

> **Peter:** *"There's not enough information on men's rights, for*

a start. Even I didn't know until recently about parental responsibility and how you don't have any rights unless you are married."

While knowledge was fairly high, misinformation was still quite extensive.

Dave: *"I read the other day that, if it takes my last name, I got rights to the baby as well. I've still got to look into it a little more, because I'm still a bit unsure."*

Andy: *"Like, from what I've heard, technically, if I wanted, if Claire got married and the baby took the father's last name, I'd have to adopt my own kid if I wanted it. Something like that: whether that's right, I don't know."*

James: *"Say me and Shannon don't work out or whatever, and she wants to get married and does, someone has got to adopt Kylie."*

One young father who sought legal advice on his particular situation found himself in a very complex legal minefield.

Jason: *"We're unmarried because she's under 18, estranged from her parents and they've got the view that they're not going to give her permission to marry me because I'm not going to stick around, without even actually taking the time to get to know me. Their opinion is that I'm a pervert and that I've got their daughter pregnant and I'm going to run off. But she's been estranged from her parents since 15 and yet they still think that they can run her life... Sarah was scared with the birth process that they were going to get involved. Because she is under 18, they are her next of kin and, if anything happened to her, because we are not married, the baby would go straight to them. Or, if they could take her to court and get custody somehow, the solicitor explained it to us that there was a possibility, so we* had to get a parental agreement out. Which means, basically, going to a solicitors, getting the forms, filling them in, taking them down to the law courts to be signed and witnessed. We both had to have identification, they are then sent to the central family unit somewhere or other and you get a contract through saying, 'I am the mother blah,blah,blah. I state that Jason Neil Friars is the father and this document gives him 50% custody, responsibility and authority over my child." Which meant that, if her parents tried to interfere, they would have to take me to court because I was the older parent, I was the official adult and somewhere along the line that also made me Sarah's next of kin because of the time we've been together she's become my common law wife, and there's now a document to say that her son is my son."

So you've now got parental rights?

"Yes, and the other thing I've got is a kind of guardianship over Sarah, which is weird because she's my fiancee and I'm responsible for her. Like, if she was arrested, because she is under 18, normally her parents would be called in, but this wouldn't happen, I'd be called in. Which is a very strange relationship."

5.2. Feelings of discrimination

All the fathers interviewed felt it unfair that they had no automatic parental rights with regard to their children.

Andy: "You've got all these women running around saying, equal rights for women, it's about time they had something for blokes... There's just no hope. Women get all the priorities, men don't get jack shit, which is really annoying."

Dave: "Some men get women pregnant and then run away, it's fair enough then. But, then, for others, like myself, who are looking forward to it, being really supportive, I don't

55

think it's right in that case if they want to help the child and what not."

One father, although his partner was in agreement, found that her mother came between him and parental rights.

James: *"And when Kylie was born and that and it came to the birth certificate, in the hospital her mum piped up and said her last name so me and Shannon didn't have a chance to say anything. And then, when we was going to register at City Hall, her mum was there and I couldn't go cos her mum was going, and so I had no say in the matter. So, basically, she had me right where she wanted me."*

When this particular relationship with his partner broke down, all contact was lost.

James: *"I ain't seeing little un no more because it was just like too complicated… I just kept getting aggravation off her mum and everything, and it just got all too much in the end."*

There was also a unanimous feeling that there was little point resorting to the courts because of the perceived bias of the likely decisions.

Andy: *"They* (mothers) *hold all the cards; the courts always find in favour of the mother and the father just loses out and everyone pretends that he doesn't exist."*

James: *"Nine times out of ten, the cases that go to court the mother seems to always get custody of the child. And sometimes that's wrong because they don't do enough homework and actually realise what's going on."*

Peter: *"The custody is normally awarded to the mother, even though the mother may not be a good influence on the child. There have been quite a few cases of that, especially*

*if it's a little girl. But I think men should get a fair chance:
if they've got a fair enough case, they should be able to have
custody of a child."*

Feelings of being discriminated against had also been raised
during the initial group interview.

Darren: *"Basically, if there's a custody battle and
everything, that doesn't mean a bloody thing. There's
nothing unless you're married."*

Paul: *"Claire looked into that, she turned round and go,
I check it out, I've got no rights whatsoever when the kid's
born unless we get married. I've got no rights whatsoever....
I mean that's another bad thing right. Women ask for equal
rights and all that sort of stuff, yeah. Where's the equal
rights bit? If the woman wants custody over a kid, they get it
just like that. Even if the father wanted the kid, sort of
thing, even if they're not married, the woman still gets it, yet
they're the ones that want equal rights and want to be
treated like a bloke. And yet they still want to have all their
separate laws for themselves, sort of thing, to have their
advantage over us, even though they want to be equal to us.
How can they say they want equal rights?"*

Two fathers had direct personal experience of legal battles for
access. One found it too much hassle and gave up.

Mick: *"I went to my solicitor and we exchanged letters to
her solicitor and that, and basically I tried, but it just wasn't
working out. So I decided to call it a day. I'm still regretting
it now. I wish I'd carried on."*

The other found the whole process got too unpleasant. The
things he had said when drunk came back to be used
against him.

Andy: "*Well, a long while back when I was really pissed out of my head down in Peppermint (Norwich Nightclub), she started getting chatted up by these blokes and I started going on to one about the baby and I turned round and said 'Right, if you don't let me see the baby, I'll take him away'. I was right out of my tree, I didn't know what I was saying and she's using that. I told my solicitor and she said, 'I'm not sure she'll use that, but thanks for letting us know', and it came back that she'd used everything that I'd said.*"

One of the mothers interviewed also had experience of the legal system, but was much more pleased with the outcome.

Jackie: "*Well, we had to go through the courts in the end cos it got messed up. He decided that he wanted Carl all the time. He took him away and we had to get a court order to get him back, and this happened last year sometime.*"

What, he just didn't return him one time?

"*No, he took him at Christmas and said he'd be back by a certain day and wasn't. So I had to go to a solicitor and get a court order to get him back and then it went through the courts so he could have him three days a week. And that's sorted out alright now.*"

Did you agree to the three days in court?

"*Yeah, cos I wanted Carl to be able to see his daddy, so he said, 'I'll have him three days a week', and we decided the days between ourselves and that's worked out fine, cos Carl gets on with his dad.*"

5.3. Attempting to set up a working arrangement

The two young men interviewed both before and after becoming a father give some interesting insights into how they attempted some resolution with their partner.

Andy:

Before birth

> "Officially, I've got no rights whatsoever, but she's just turned around and said, if I want to see the baby, I can see the baby. We'll be working everything out together, anyway, what the name's going to be, eh, what we are going to do with it, everything is going to be with both of us working it out. Basically, it's like I'm married to her — all the access I want."

After birth and break-up of relationship

> "When we were together, she said 'If we ever split up, however bad it's been, you can see him as much as you like' and all sorts, and what happened to that (despairing laughter)? 'No matter how we finish, whether it's bad or good, you can see him whenever you want,' it just didn't happen."

Dave:

Before birth

> "I got very little, or no, rights over the kid unless Joanne agrees to sign, and she's already said she would, a joint parental agreement."

So, she is happy to sign for joint responsibility?

> "Yeah, I believe so, but whether she does at the time is going to be another matter. I hope she does. It's more for security for myself, really."

After birth

"So far I haven't got a parental agreement, which I still want desperately... She thinks I might be slippery and get around her and, as soon as I got that done, I'd leave her. When we got the birth certificate done, Joanne was a bit dubious about it and was paranoid about it straight afterwards because she thought, now he's got my last name, I've got rights to him and I'd leave him, but I've proved her wrong on that one."

6. An overview of research findings

The intention of this book was to investigate the experiences, feelings and attitudes of young, unmarried fathers — and the mothers of their children — towards fatherhood. As the sample interviewed was relatively small and all interviewees came from the same geographical area, the following summary is offered not as necessarily relating to all young unmarried fathers, but as an insight into the experiences, feelings, attitudes and beliefs of a particular group.

6.1 Being a young father

One of the clearest findings of the research was that, contrary to the stereotype that a young father's first impulse is to walk away from their parental responsibilities, there was a real desire, on the part of the fathers, to be involved in the care and nurturing of their own children. The stereotype of young fathers as uncaring and uninvolved males is not always true. Given the opportunity to take a part in the caring for and nurturing of their child, many of them report that the fathering experience is a central event in their young lives. Francke's 1978 study in Robinson (1988) on abortion highlights the dilemma for young men when they find themselves in circumstances beyond their control and have difficulty in expressing their feelings — and sometimes no opportunity to do so. Francke further suggests that it seems ironic that, while many women, when they become pregnant, feel themselves to be helpless victims of sexual passion (partner stronger than they were) or of fate (malfunction of contraceptive), the situation is reversed when women leave the fathers out of the decision-making as to the outcome of the pregnancy. It is then the men's turn to feel trapped and helpless.

The interview data revealed that, although apprehensive, the young fathers wanted to play a part and contribute to the decision-making and planning concerning their female partners and babies. Many of the sample were emerging as young men who wanted to be active fathers and, when given the opportunity, were involved in raising their children. When there was an opportunity to be involved, daily contact was often maintained, financial contributions made and there was participation in decisions about the child's welfare. The fact that sharing in the nurturing was not always part of their experience seemed to have more to do with the reluctance on the part of the child's mother for the father to play a significant role than hesitancy on the part of the father. As other recent studies (Speak, Cameron & Gilroy 1997) have shown, it is not that young fathers abandon their children, but that social agencies, peers, the mother's family and even the mother herself abandon the young fathers.

Fatherhood was seen by many of those interviewed not as something to run away from, but as the source of a sense of pride. And this attitude was maintained even when there was overt hostility from the young mother's family. Considerable evidence came from the interviews that the maternal grandparents often acted as gatekeepers, barring the young father access to his child. Considerable stress was felt by a young father at being left out of the decisions being made by the mother and her parents about his child.

Fatherhood was also recognised as a role that carried certain responsibilities. A strong desire was expressed by the young fathers to "be there for your child" and to be a good and responsible father. The significance of regular contact was frequently mentioned, and regret was expressed when contact had been reduced or even lost. This loss of contact was often linked with conflict with the young mother and her family. The desire to be worthwhile fathers themselves was often contrasted with the young men's less than satisfactory experiences with their own fathers.

My findings relate closely to those of the American Psychological Association (1985, quoted in Robinson 1988):

> Most people think that teenage fathers' first impulse is to walk away from their parental responsibilities. In books and movies they are portrayed as self-centred ne'er-do-wells, interested only in sexual gratification, who have fleeting, casual relationships with their girl friends and hit the road at the first hint of pregnancy. But our research and others' shows that many young men go through the same emotional struggle and confusion that young mothers do........
> Teenage fathers often want babies as much as teenage mothers do, for many of the same reasons. A child may be the first thing in their young lives that seems truly theirs. For those performing poorly at school, caring for a baby may be their first tangible accomplishment. For those reared in troubled homes, the infant may be the first human from whom they can receive love... They have strong emotional ties with their girlfriends and demonstrate genuine concern for their babies.... (although) teenage fathers who stay in the picture often face unbridled hostility from their girlfriends' families.

It also became clear during the interviews that young fathers, like young mothers, are faced with substantial obstacles to being satisfactory parents. These obstacles include the impact on employment of the interruption of education or job/career preparation, as well as economic disadvantage. In spite of these hurdles, some do succeed as parents, but others fail to receive the support that would help them in surmounting the obstacles they face.

The young women interviewed also thought that fatherhood was important but, having had negative experiences with their own fathers, did not want such experiences repeated with their own children. Both young mothers and young fathers indicated, in contradiction to the assumptions of some feminist writers (e.g. Greer 1986), that they would really like a more conventional family structure. However, this did not necessarily mean that they saw the child's father as capable of playing a significant father role in such a traditional family set-up.

6.2 Being an unemployed father

Recent changes in Britain's occupational structure have reduced the employment opportunities for young men to support families that were available to them 20 years ago. Unemployment among young men has risen and the rate of employment among young fathers is considerably higher than it is for young men who do not have children. For example, almost half of the 20-24 year old fathers in the 1992 B.H.P.S. were unemployed. This was three times the rate for young men in this age group who were not fathers, many of whom would have been students.

Young fathers are often caught in a cycle of economic hardship. As Kieran (in Burghes, Clarke and Cronin,1997) says:

...men who become fathers when they are young run greater risks of social and economic disadvantage and are more likely themselves to have come from families which experienced financial hardship.

This cycle can, as Burghes (in Burghes, Clarke and Cronin, 1997) suggests, extend to the next generation:

Young unemployed fathers lack the status that employment bestows and are unable to make financial provision for their children. Unemployment may also reduce the likelihood of young mothers and fathers forming residential parent partnerships.

Contrary to popular myth, most of the unemployed unmarried fathers interviewed for this research had a desire to work. Mick, reflecting the feelings of the majority, said:

"It's personal satisfaction. Instead of signing on for it you've actually gone out there and earnt it... it is boring sitting on your bum all day, just waiting for the fortnight to come and sign your name and get your money. And it isn't worth being branded, you know, because you're on the dole, that's it, you know... We're not all bums on the social. Some of us do have direction."

Not surprisingly, the financial implications of being unemployed were uppermost in many of the fathers' minds. For a number, the need to exist on a very low income was deeply worrying. Many of those interviewed had had to learn to make tough decisions in order to be able to live within their limited budgets. They further recognised that poverty meant that they could not provide for their children as they wanted, nor were they in a position to establish and maintain a cohabiting relationship and a home. They felt strongly that their economic situation prevented them from reaching standards met by others, and that this in turn negatively affected the way that they were perceived. For example, a number of young fathers felt that they had been rejected by their partner's family because of their unemployed status. They felt they were being solely judged on their ability to bring in a wage.

> **James:** "*The reason she (partner's mother) sort of don't want me being about is to do with the fact that I'm not working. I don't fit her standards.*"

> **Mick:** "*I'm not a man, I'm just a boy in a man's shell... Your father says you're a man if you do this, you're a man if you go out and earn a crust and bring it home.*"

In addition to feeling discriminated against in the job market, some felt that they were also suffering from the disappearance of many traditional 'working class' jobs.

> **Peter:** "*Most of the industries I've worked in have been battered over the last few years*".

Because of this loss of opportunity, some felt devalued because they believed their skills were of little use in the current labour market, and others felt stuck in an employment rut.

> **Mick:** "*With me, it's just that I've been stuck in the same kind of work, I want to broaden my horizons and try something different.*"

Whilst, clearly, unemployment was almost entirely viewed in negative terms, some positive aspects in relation to being a father were identified. This further illustrates the importance that these young men attached to fatherhood. One young father expressed the opinion that a period of unemployment should be compulsory for all new fathers.

Peter: *"I think everyone should be made unemployed for six months after a baby's been born."*

Why's that?

"So that they know how damn hard it is."

Another of the young fathers interviewed specifically took a part-time job so that he could spend more time with his son.

Stephen: *"That suits us down to the ground because I only work from eight till one, so most of the time is spent with my kid."*

While another had given up a part-time job to be more supportive to his partner.

Dave: *"I got a job recently and had to give it up because Joanne just couldn't cope on her own. I think she was having a nervous breakdown at the time and so I had to come home and look after the baby and that."*

6.3 Being an unmarried father

Current legislation gives an unmarried mother sole parental rights and responsibilities, whilst giving the father only the financial responsibility for his child. Even this responsibility is not conferred automatically on unmarried fathers, as The Children's Act sought to protect vulnerable unmarried mothers. This legislation is not always widely understood. An article in *Childright* (May 1998) pointed out that:

it appears that many people simply assume that an unmarried father has parental responsibility, especially if the mother and father have jointly registered the child's birth.

My research found that, while some of the unmarried fathers understood the legal situation, this was not true of all of them.

Dave: *"I read the other day that, if it takes my last name, I've got rights to the baby as well. I've still got to look into it a little more, because I'm still a bit unsure."*

Peter: *"There's not enough information on men's rights, for a start. Even I didn't know until recently about parental responsibility and how you don't have any rights unless you are married."*

Parental responsibility may be important to some people as a symbol of the legal status of parenthood, but the possession of parental responsibility probably has little or no effect on a father's role in the day-to-day upbringing of his child. That is at least while the parents are living together or co-operating in their arrangements for the children. For the majority of unmarried fathers, the lack of parental responsibility does not become an issue until the relationship with the mother breaks down, or until the mother becomes unable to exercise her parental responsibility through, say, accident or illness.

It can be a particular source of grievance for some unmarried fathers that they may be forced to support their children financially, whether or not they have acquired parental responsibility under the Children's Act. However, as already stated, the Children's Act does not automatically confer parental responsibility on unmarried fathers, especially when children have been born as a result of violent or coercive relationships. This, again, can be resented by some young unmarried fathers.

Andy: *"Officially, I've got no rights whatsoever."*

Dave: *"I got little, or no, rights over the kid unless Joanne agrees to sign."*

Darren: *"You've got nothing unless you're married. Like there's, urm, parental responsibility and that lot."*

This lack of recognition of fatherhood obviously upset many of the young men interviewed, hence I agree with Speak, Cameron & Gilroy (1997):

> *We need fundamental reform of this legislation which will give legal recognition to the importance of fatherhood... We should ask what messages the current situation gives out about the importance of a father's involvement, when it does not even afford cohabiting fathers equal rights with the mother.... Even if legislation cannot be changed, there is a need for a wide reaching education programme to inform single fathers of the current situation and to encourage more to seek rights under the current legislation.*

Feelings of being discriminated against in law were raised during the initial group interview. There was unanimous agreement that there was little point resorting to the courts because of the anticipated bias in the decisions that would be taken there. Two of those interviewed had direct personal experience of legal battles for access. One had found it too much hassle and had given up.

> **Mick:** *"I went to my solicitor and we exchanged letters to her solicitor, and that, and basically it wasn't working out. So I decided to call it a day. I'm still regretting it now. I wish I'd carried on."*

Rhoden and Robinson (in Hawkins & Dollahite 1997) identify the feeling of intimidation from the courts as a key factor in preventing them from participating in the care of their children:

Young fathers express care for the health and welfare of the mother and baby as well as concern about being able to support the mother and child financially... They often feel estranged from participation by understandable, yet unbridled hostility from their girlfriends' fathers, <u>intimidation from the courts</u>, and neglect from the social services agencies (my underlining)

Despite the difficulties facing them, the interviews demonstrated that some of the young fathers made a real attempt to set up a working arrangement with their partners. This is particularly illustrated by the responses of two of the young men.

Andy:

Before birth

"Officially, I've got no rights whatsoever, but she's just turned around and said if I want to see the baby, I can see the baby. We'll be working everything out together, anyway, what the name's going to be, er, what we are going to do with it — everything is going to be with both of us working it out. Basically, it's like I'm married to her — all the access I want."

After birth and break-up of relationship

"When we were together she said, 'If we ever split up, however bad it's been, you can see him as much as you like' and all sorts, and what happened to that (despairing laughter)? *'No matter how we finish, whether it's bad or good, you can see him whenever you want.'* It just didn't happen."

70

Dave:

Before birth

"I got little, or no, rights over the kid unless Joanne agrees to sign, and she's already said she would, a joint parental agreement."

So, she is happy to sign for joint responsibility?

"Yeah, I believe so, but whether she does at the time is going to be another matter. I hope she does, it's more security for myself, really."

After birth

"So far, I haven't got a parental agreement, which I still want desperately... She thinks I might be slippery and get around her and as soon as I got that done I'd leave her. When we got the birth certificate done, Joanne was a bit dubious about it and was paranoid about it straight afterwards because she thought, now he's got my last name. I've got rights to him and I'd leave him, but I've proved her wrong there."

However, as the excerpts from their interviews show, the situation that the young fathers find themselves in with regard to their children is far from ideal as far as they are concerned. Lack of resolution and uncertainty with regard to contact and participation in care is likely to have a disruptive effect, not only on the parents involved, but the child as well. The emotional costs of an unsatisfactory resolution may also be a factor in failing or limited contact. The effort to maintain contact in a 'hostile climate' may prove to be too demanding emotionally, not only for the fathers, but, as they see it, for their children, and, if they exist, new partners. There are also no established norms for unmarried fathers. Blankenhorn

(1995) notes that we have not yet evolved a set of powerful cultural norms around what it means to be a good father for a man outside a committed relationship with the mother and a breadwinner role for the children. He further believes that the lack of appropriate cultural norms is partly due to increased individualism and a decrease in community expectations of private behaviour. Thus unmarried and non-resident fathers are free to create their own way of being a father, even if the result is neglect. My own research indicates that this neglect can be further confounded by the obstacles that unmarried fathers often find in the way of them attempting good parenting.

7. Recommendations for practice

The implications of this research are that much needs to change, including, as expressed in the last chapter, change in the legislation concerning the status of unmarried fathers.

However, what I want to focus on here is the need for a radical re-examination and restructuring of a wide range of services, particularly those within health, education, social services and the voluntary sector. Deep-seated prejudices will have to be honestly faced and policies put in place to actively encourage the involvement, support and education of young fathers.

I will make some brief suggestions under four headings — access to advice, improved training of professionals, improved educational opportunities for young men and improved access options.

7.1. Access to advice

Clear information for mothers and fathers about their and their children's legal position.

There is a general ignorance with regard to legal matters and legislation concerning parenthood. This is very different from American schooling, where The American Constitution and Legislation is part of the curriculum. The legal language clearly needs unpacking for people, otherwise the whole legal system can appear even more threatening. There is an enormous need for clearly-expressed leaflets and for advice centres specifically for young people, as many young parents live under misapprehensions as to what the law is.

Knowledge of where they can get advice over legal issues

Centres where advice over legal matters can be obtained must be accessible, with approachable staff. These centres need to be well-advertised in places where young parents go. Information needs to be written in accessible language and attractively presented.

7.2. Improved Training

Training for those involved in the legal professions

Education of all those involved in the legal process about the importance of continuing the bond with the father is clearly much needed. Attitudes in courts that young children are always best with their mother (women's role, what women do naturally, etc.), and that young unmarried fathers are feckless, still persist. Training should include a consideration of the nature of fathering, some of the insights into the importance of children maintaining contact with both parents and the importance of being an effective father for the esteem of the young father himself.

In-service education for those professionals working with young people

When many of today's practising professionals were trained, the available research on young fathers was thin, as any review of the literature will demonstrate. Since I began my research, I have noticed an increasing interest in this area and a growth of material to counter the myth of the disinterested young father.

If professionals are not to continue with unhelpful perspectives on what the attitudes and beliefs of young fathers are likely to be, there is a great need for in-service education focused on young fathers. This focus is as necessary for those working with young women, as well as young men. The professionals' attitudes to the role of the father can easily be picked up by young women or serve to amplify their existing negative attitudes.

Academic and professional courses for those about to work with young people

It is essential that courses targeted at those about to work with young people should take cognisance of the research into the attitudes and beliefs of young fathers. Library provision and student reading lists need to be examined to ensure that recent literature on young fathers is included and promoted. Especially when courses have a long history, it is important to ensure that the material presented is up to date and that, when literature reflects outdated views, this should be drawn to the attention of students (the work of Bowlby and Freud would be such examples).

7.3. Education of young people

The School Curriculum

The consideration of family life and parenting as part of the school curriculum is always likely to be a contested area. Individual value positions come to the fore when the content of such teaching is discussed.

However, it is clear that teaching about family and parenting is high on the present Government's agenda. There is always concern that any input into the school curriculum on families will appear to devalue certain family arrangements. Perhaps a starting point can be the best interest of the child, and this 'best interest' needs to acknowledge the variety of family contexts in which children find themselves. It was interesting to note from my interviews that several young fathers expressed a desire to do the best for their children, often accompanied by the comment that this could hardly be said of their own fathers. When considering parenting, there is a great need for the role of the father to be explored, not in a sexist sense, but in terms of what fathers as individuals can contribute to the rearing of their children. Health education courses and Education for Citizenship provide opportunities for family life and parenting to be included within the current structure of the school curriculum.

Separate groups for fathers and mothers

Sex education classes in schools have indicated that there can be value in having separate groups of males and females, at least for part of a course. There is some indication that males do not like losing face in front of females, and therefore will not ask questions about things that concern them. The sexes also may wish to ask different questions. It may be appropriate, therefore, to have some fathering classes for males only and similar female only groups.

The informal curriculum of Youth and Community Education

A constant criticism of the idea of including family life and parenting in the formal school curriculum has been the inappropriateness of school as an arena for learning about personal and social issues. The more informal context of youth and community education allows for a variety of views to be expressed, questions asked without fear of humiliation and for a more open discussion to take place. However, the non-compulsory nature of community education means that not all will take part. The task for community education would therefore be to make such programmes attractive and accessible. If people could be encouraged to attend, the ethos of community education should provide a sympathetic context for value positions to be explained and individuals helped to come to their own informed value positions.

Parent preparation classes

There has been a considerable growth and emphasis on parenting classes in recent times. It is true that there has been some encouragement for men to attend ante natal classes run by local hospitals and groups like the National Childbirth Trust. However, there is a big lack of take-up from young, unmarried, unemployed men.

There is an off-putting perception of 'middle classness' about such provision to a young, unmarried, unemployed father, and greater energy and understanding needs to be injected if this group is to be properly represented. If parenting classes are to be attended by young, unmarried, unemployed men, care needs to be taken as to the venue, timing and the approach taken.

Literature will need to be more inclusive, as well as clear and attractive. Young fathers need to be encouraged to talk and express their concerns and not to feel they are being lectured at. More fathers should be involved in the delivery of such classes to give young men more confidence to speak and greater insight into the expectations of the role.

Support groups for young fathers

There are a wide range of successful projects offering valuable support and education to young mothers throughout the country. However, projects that work with young fathers are unfortunately extremely rare.

In an attempt to respond to requests from young fathers themselves seeking support in looking after their children, M.A.P. set up a weekly young fathers group which has now been running for over four years. This group, facilitated by two fathers, has proved invaluable in raising confidence, as well as in addressing emotional and practical concerns. The work, however, has existed on a shoestring budget as, until very recently, few funders have seen it as an area worthy of funding.

I would like to see a network of such groups develop across the whole country and good practice shared.

7.4. Improved Access

Increased accessibility of more parent-and-child groups

Many unemployed young people have limited living conditions. This can make it difficult to provide adequate play facilities for a child. There has undoubtedly been an increase in parent and child groups around the country, but many young fathers perceive that they would not be welcome and lack the confidence to access them. Stories abound of being met with stony silence and being left outside any activities. Clearly, much work needs to be done to improve access opportunities and create a more supportive, welcoming atmosphere.

If a young father did not have good play experiences himself, this sort of provision can prove essential if he is going to learn to relate in a meaningful way with his child.

The provision of facilities for good access experiences

One of the major problems for a non-custodial parent is a suitable venue for providing good access experiences. This can be especially difficult if the mother and father live at some distance from each other, or their accommodation is limited or shared. The expense of a hotel room, or even the cost of buying food at a cafe or restaurant, can be beyond the means of someone unemployed or on a low wage. There is an important role for agencies to provide facilities for parents to meet and play with their children. This can be especially useful if a level of supervision is required.

A number of imaginative projects have been initiated, for instance 'Dads and lads' is a Y.M.C.A. initiative where young fathers can engage with their children in a sporting context.

Summary

It is clear from the words of the young, unemployed, unmarried fathers interviewed that there is a great need for supporting unmarried fathers in their attempts to be good parents.

Other research evidence, such as Furstenberg's (1976 in Robinson 1988), would suggest that when young fathers actively participate in their children's development, the children are less likely to have behavioural problems. In contrast, when young fathers are absent, their children are more likely to have behavioural problems, lower self-esteem and trust levels, and, in general, show poor social competence.

What more pressing reasons could there be for initiating reform?

Appendix

i. Research Methodology

When I started the research for an M.Ed. at U.E.A. that would form the backbone of this book, I had no idea that I would end up focusing on fatherhood. In fact, at the time, I had an inclination to focus on the area of unemployed young people and spirituality.

However, I wanted the research to be as 'field led' as possible, and for the key issues to come out of initial unstructured interviews. So, to identify possible key issues, I set up a series of individual interviews and a group interview.

The research methodology chosen was that of a case study whereby I carried out a series of loosely or semi-structured interviews with the young people. Such qualitative interviews are frequently referred to as 'conversations with a purpose'.

I asked the young people to talk about their lives, what was important to them, what their hopes were, what issues they felt strongly about and so on. All the interviews lasted between 30 and 50 minutes.

After completing the interviews, I listened closely to all the tapes for a key 'field led' theme that I would pursue in greater depth. Several issues, potentially worthy of follow-up emerged, including issues of sexuality, spirituality and the experience of those that have never had paid employment. However, the issue that came through most frequently, clearly and consistently was that of parenthood, particularly fatherhood. This concern with fatherhood was located in the context of being unmarried in all of the sample interviewed.

The decision to focus on this group of young men led to the setting up of a second set of individual interviews to explore further the experience and beliefs related to fatherhood, especially in relation to parallel experiences of being young, unemployed and unmarried. Following the initial interviews, I decided that I would gain a wider perspective on fatherhood in this context if I also included interviews with young unemployed, unmarried mothers.

My research journey could, therefore, be summarised as follows:

a) Decision to focus on experience and beliefs of young unemployed men;

b) Loosely-structured individual interviews with 17 young men and five young women and a group interview with 6 young men;

c) Fatherhood identified as a key issue;

d) Semi-structured interviews with seven young men and three young women to explore experience and beliefs relating to fatherhood, with special reference to being young, unemployed and unmarried.

The nature of the investigation was clearly potentially very sensitive. I therefore took great care to make sure I got the informed consent of all of those taking part.

Each young person first volunteered to take part in an interview and then was asked if they objected to me tape recording the interview. At the end, they were given the opportunity to listen back to the tape and point out anything they did not want me to use. I also said they could check, and amend if necessary, the transcribed interview when I had typed it up. I promised to change all names mentioned in the interview in an attempt to maintain confidentiality. I also promised to change some minor details (such as which hostel they lived in, for example) to make it hard for them to be identified or traced. I explained that I would use nothing of what they said 'off the record' when the tape recorder was switched off. I stated that the research would be available publicly and that I would attempt to get the work published. I made it clear that they were giving me the right to use the data generated through the interview in ways which I saw fit. I also explained that they could withdraw their consent at any stage, keep the audio-tape, and, if required, I would not use a single word of their particular interview.

ii. Bibliography

Biller, H.B. and Solomon, R.S. (1986) *Child maltreatment and paternal deprivation: A manifesto for research, prevention, and treatment*. Lexington, MA: Lexington Books.

Blackenhorn, D. (1995) *Fatherless America*. New York: Basic Books.

Bowlby, J. (1952) *Maternal Care and Mental Health & Deprivation of Maternal Care (Two volumes in one)*. New York: Schocken Books.

Burgess, A. (1997) *Fatherhood Reclaimed*. London: Vermilion.

Burghes, L., Clarke, L. & Cronin, N. (1997) *Fathers and Fatherhood in Britain. Occasional Paper 23*. London: Family

Policy Studies Centre.

C.A.B. (1996) Basic Information pack. London: N.A.C.A.B.

Childright (May 1998 No. 146) *'Paternity and Parental Responsibilty for Unmarried Fathers.'*

Clarke, L., Condy, A. & Downing, A. (1995) *'Fathers: a socio-demographic profile. Report to Department of Health.'* London: Family Policy Studies Centre Working Paper, 1997.

Freud, A. (1991) *The essentials of psycho-analysis.* Harmondsworth: Penguin.

Greer, G. (1986) *The madwoman's underclothes.* London: Picador.

Hawkins, A.J. & Dollahite, D.C. Eds (1997) *Generative Fathering: Beyond deficit perspectives.* London: Thousand Oaks, Calif.

Hudson, F. & Ineichen, B. (1991). *Taking It Lying Down: Sexuality and teenage motherhood.* Basingstoke: MacMillan Education.

Murray, C. (1990) *The Emerging British Underclass. Choices in Welfare Series No.2.* London: IEA Health and Welfare Unit.

Phares, V. (1996) *Conducting nonsexist research, prevention and treatment with fathers and mothers: a call for change.* Psychology of women quarterly, 20.

Robinson, B.E. (1988) *Teenage fathers.* Massachusetts: Lexington books.

Silverstein, L.B. (1996) 'Fathering is a Feminist Issue.' *Psychology of women quarterly, 20.*

Speak, S., Cameron, S. & Gilroy, R. (1997) *Young Single Fathers: participation in fatherhood-barriers and bridges.* London: Family Policy Studies Centre

Working with Men is a not-for-profit organisation that supports the development of work with men through resources, publications, training, consultancy and advice. We have a network of trainers and consultants with substantial experience of working with men.

What we do

WWM carries out projects on important issues related to men, including fatherhood, relationships, mental health, sexual health, violence and growing up.

WWM offers a consultancy service, which provides research, project evaluations, strategy papers, training programmes, and workers supervision schemes to a broad range of organisations.

WWM produces a quarterly journal that keeps practitioners, students and policy makers informed of developments in practice, emerging key debates, and reviews of books, publications and resources helpful to those developing work with men.

WWM offers a regular training programme, as well as tailor-made courses for a wide range of statutory and voluntary organisations.

WWM also produce games, packs, posters, videos and other educational materials for use with boys, young and older men.

WWM applies alone and with other organisations for grants from charitable trusts; is invited to carry out major reviews and development work for statutory organisations; uses its own reserves to research and develop areas of work thought to be of importance (but that funders are currently not interested in).

How to contact **Working With Men**

All correspondence to: 320 Commercial Way, London SE15 1QN
For consultancy and training: 0171-732-9409 (phone & fax)
e-mail: treflloyd@aol.com
Website: http:/www.stejonda.demon.co.uk/wwm/